Poetry from the Heart

By Kathrine Niffen

Poetry from the Heart

Katharine L Niffen

Published by Katharine L Niffen, 2021.

While every precaution has been taken in the preparation of this book, the publisher assumes no responsibility for errors or omissions, or for damages resulting from the use of the information contained herein.

POETRY FROM THE HEART

First edition. May 27, 2021.

ISBN: 979-8201335175

Written by Katharine L Niffen.

This book is a work of fiction names,characters,business,events and incidents are the product of the author imagination and any resemblance to actual persons living or dead or actual events is purely confidential

This book is full of poetry of all kinds. But all form my heart. It has sadness,love,and desire.With a few that I hope will make you laugh.

This book is dedicated to my son and his family. For always being there supporting me in my writing. And believing in me.It's also in the honor of my mom and dad. Who will always be with me in my heart. Love you both.

It's also dedicated to my best friends and their family. Who became my family.For being patient with me as I bugged them through the whole process.Alone with supporting me in my dreams.

I want you all to know I love you all.And thank each and everyone of you. For you all mean the world to me

Love you

Table of contents

When I look at you

I see that you are voluptuous
　　Plan out flawless
　　That you are a rare Pearl
　　In the sea
　　With your enticing lips
　　And your flirtatious eyes
　　With your seductive was
　　For you are a flower among thorns

The pain I feel because of you

It started small
    And grew large all because of you
    Won't let me touch you
    Won't let me near you
    Hurting to kiss you
    Hurting to be with you
    My heart is breaking
    Needing your love
    My stomach is in knots
    Wanting to hear your voice
    My hands are hurting
    Needing to hold you
    Hurting all over
    For loving you

The way I feel about you

I can't stop thinking about you
    I have lecherousness for you
    Adultery is all ready on my mind
    My feelings are unbridled
    It's down right sinful
    It's entirely raw
    Along with heartfelt and honest
    AS it is uncontrollably
    It's a raw element
    It's furiously passionate.
    It's a brutal hungry I can't satisfy
    It's insatiable
    The way I feel is profoundly,insane
    It's pure and reckless
    It's simple and extrollable hot
    It's crazy uncontrollable hot
    Along with physical
    It's complete and overpowering
    It's taboo and healthy
    I've been keeping it all pent up
    It's bittersweet and cynical
    It's devilish and wholesome
    I want to leave all the consequence behind
    When I'm thinking about you

If I die

If I die tonight
    Would you noticed
    Would you be sad
    Would you cry
    Would you miss me
    If I died
    Would it change your life
    Would you even care
    Would it break your heart
    Would you think of me
    If I died
    Would you look at my pictures
    Would you talk about me
    Would you remember the good times we had
    Would you go to my funeral
    If I died
    What would you do

The future

The future is getting shorter
    Don't know if I will make it through the night
    It's getting too late to live my dream
    I might of lost my chance
    To love you,to hold you
    I'm afraid I lost you forever
    I could be taking my last breath
    My last though would be of you
    Of how it could of been
    Your a million dollars
    A model in my eyes
    The future is dark
    Life is short
    I will be lucky if I live through the year
    THat's the only thing that is real

Hate

It started out small
    Then it began to grow
    It's eating up my soul
    It's taking over ever thought
    I can't stop it
    It took ahold of me
    Now it's stronger than me
    I see no way out
    I can' control it
    No wonder it spreads
    To everyone I know
    It's like a deadly virus
    That's there is no cure
    I pray for redemption
    I hope for change
    Before it's to late
    And the hate destroys me

You

You feed my heart
　　You feed my soul
　　You make me grow in ways
　　I never imagined
　　You build me up
　　You showed me how to reach
　　For the stars
　　You pushed me to dream
　　You pushed me to desire
　　You never let me give up
　　You showed me how to love
　　You showed me how to care
　　You showed me what life is all about

What if

What if
     I grabbed you
     And kissed you long and hard
     Held you tight in my arms
     Showed you how you should be loved
     Would you fight me
     Or would you embrace me or kiss me back
     OR even hold me close
     Would you give yourself to me
     What if
     I could give you everything your heart desires
     What if
     I'm the one you're supposed to be with
     Your one and only soulmate
     What if
     I'm the one you're looking for
     The one your soul aces to be with
     The one you dream of at night

My Christmas wish

I wish that this christmas
    You would see
    What is right in front of you
    The one who's been loving you
    For all these years
    I wish that this christmas
    That you would feel how I feel about you
    The pain that I go through
    Not being able to have you
    I wish that this christmas
    That you would love me
    The way I love you
    That you would desire me
    The way I desire you
    I wish that this christmas
    Would be the one
    Where you come running into my arms
    I wish that this christmas
    You will tell me you love me to
    That you want to be with me
    I wish that this christmas
    You will say yes
    When I get down on one knee
    And ask you to marry me
    This is my christmas wish

I'm going crazy

I'm going crazy missing my baby
    I love looking into them bedroom eyes
    Kissing them sweet lips
    Miss hearing the way you say my name
    The way you held me tight
    I'm going crazy missing my baby
    The way you made me laugh
    The way you make me feel
    Your my one and only
    The one I can't stop dreaming of
    Your the love of my life
    I'm going crazy missing my baby
    The one who fills my soul
    Your the one I live for
    Your the one I fight for
    I' going crazy missing my baby

The Thoughts

I set here all alone
   Can't get the thoughts out of my mind
   Knowing I'm disposable
   That I'm nothing special to anyone
   My heart beats a mile a minute
   My mind is going crazy
   Should I do it or should I not
   Is the question that runs in my head
   Wondering if they would even notice I'm gone
   Knowing it's all a lie
   Wondering why my mind treats me this way
   My heart feels one way
   My mind feels another
   Am I'm going insane
   Wondering if everyone else is going through the same
   Trying to hold my head up high
   Doing all I can to fight these insane thoughts
   Going on in my mind

Trouble when I first saw you

I knew you was trouble
     But I couldn't stay away
     There was something about you
     That drove me crazy
     You was changing me
     From the time we meet
     I don't know what to do
     Just know I can't stay away from you
     I was a good girl
     But not any more
     Living on the edge
     Hanging out with you
     Freaking my family out
     As they wounding what's happening to me
     Living the wildlife with you
     And loving every minute of it

My mistake

Laying in a hospital bed
    Wounding where it all went wrong
    Wearing my heart on my sleeve
    Fighting for my life
    Living on a machine
    Can't open my eyes or say a word
    Hoping you are praying for my soul
    Can't believe I was so stupid
    To do this to everyone
    What was I thinking
    Destroying everyone I know
    Ripping apart their hearts demolishing their souls
    Because I was a fool
    When I tried to take my own life
    Believing I wasn't lovedI was blind to see
    What was before me
    Now I pray that you will forgive me
    And keep on loving me
    As much as I love you

My mistake, My love

I texted behind your back
    Had my secret calls
    I snuck around every chance I got
    I flirted with others
    Never meant to hurt you
    It was my stupidity
    I made out with several other people
    I din't think about what I was doing
    I don't want to lose you
    I promise I will never do it again
    I know what I did wrong and I can't apologize enough
    I never loved any of them
    Your the only one I want
    Your the only one I love
    I promise you today it will never happen again
    I don't want to lose you
    I can't live without you
    I love you and no one else
    Forgive me for being a dumass
    Please don't leave me your my heart and soul
    My one and only Baby I love you

Dream mate

I close my eyes
    And I see you ,and hear you
    I can feel your touch

I can smell you close
You become alive to me
And make all my dreams come true
You fill all my fantasies
Wishing it was real, needing it to be real
Your blue eyes and long hair
Sexy legs and your tight ads,and firm butt
The way you hold me in your arms
The sensitive way you kiss me
The animalistic way you love me
THe way you cuddle me at night
Your my dream mate the reason I sleep
I just can't stay away from you
Praying you would love me for real
Making all my dreams come true

My Juliet

Why you gotta look like that
　　You got my heart a jumping
　　My blood a boiling
　　Oh Juliet forget about Romeo
　　He don't have nothing on me
　　I will wine and dine you
　　Romance you like no other
　　I don't want your man
　　Your the one I desire
　　You stole my heart
　　With just one look
　　Now you got me hooked
　　You'll never find another
　　I'm one of a kind
　　So come on Juliet
　　Let's run away together
　　Won't you be my Juliet
　　My true love

My Redneck life

I'm a redneck woman
    Loving them country boys
    I know what they can do
    Showing them city boys up
    When their loving you
    I'm loving this redneck life
    Parting with my country boys
    Spending my nights along a bonfire
    Drinking whiskey and listing to country music
    Just parting the night away
    Loving my pick up truck
    Having bar room fights
    Doing some line dancing
    Going hunting with my dog
    Loving my redneck life
    Hanging with my country boys
    What a sweet life it is
    A country boy on each arm
    Whiskey filling the fridge
    Grilling on the barbecue
    Nothing like a redneck life
    So sweet and pure
    What a life to live
    I'm just a redneck woman
    Loving some country boys
    Loving my redneck life

Hunting on my mind

Got hunting on my mind
    Looking for that special prey
    He's a beast like no other
    He's clever and sneaky
    Often hiding among us
    Who's got a knockout smile
    And dreamy blue eyes
    Abs of steel
    Can destroy me with a kiss
    Got hunting on my mind
    Looking for the man of my dreams
    A hard-working loving man
    That knows how to love
    A bad country girl
    A whiskey drinking party loving man
    A rare man to find
    A truck driving dog loving man
    Who can set me on fire
    With a single touch
    A dangerous man
    The perfect dream man
    Got hunting on my mind
    Needing the perfect man

My love

He's my stud muffin
    She's my sweet honey bun
    Don't know which one to choose
    Loving them both
    It's so different
    Their so sweet
    Just can't get enough
    LOving me in different ways
    Driving me crazy
    Making me choose
    Don't want to lose either one
    He's the man of my dreams
    She's the woman that fills my fantasies
    Needing them both
    He's my baby
    She's my sweetheart
    Can't love without weather one
    Needing their love
    They take me to paradise
    When they hold me tight
    Afraid of losing them
    He's my sweet loving man
    She's my tender loving woman
    How can I choose
    When I'm in love with them both
    He's my stud muffin
    She's my sweet honey bun
    They're the love of my life
    Who I can't live without

My love for you

I come to you on bended knee
    To spill my soul to you
    The way you make me feel
    My heart breaks into a million pieces
    Afraid of what you would think of me
    For the way I feel about you
    You got my heads spinning
    My heart a racing
    And my mind going crazy
    All because I can't stop thinking of you
    Hoping you would feel the same
    Praying you wouldn't break my heart
    It would destroy my soul
    All because I fell deeply in love with you
    So now I'm on bended knee
    Pouring out my soul to you
    Telling you just how much you mean to me
    And I can not live with out you in my life
    For all I want from you is to be my wife

My sweet and pure love

The love I have for you
 Is like no other
 Your my forbidden love
 The one I can only have in my dreams
 Where there is no end to our magic
 Where the world is all ours
 Where our love is cherished
 Where our fantasies become real
 Where our desires are forfilled
 Our kisses are sweet and pure
 Our love is one of a kind
 Our love never dies
 Holding each other tight and never letting go
 Never wanting it to end
 Never wanting to wake up
 Don't want to miss your kisses
 Don't want to miss your touch
 Don't want to miss your sweet love
 Coe fall into my arms
 Let's hold each other tight
 Let's make these dreams come true
 Let's show the world true love
 A love so sweet and pure
 A love like no other
 A love that grows stronger by the minute
 A love that moves mountains
 A love that waters the sea
 Your my forbidden love
 Your my forbidden fruit

One that I can not ignore
You are the one my heart burns for
The one my soul has been searching for
You are my sweet pure love

Covid - 19

You came In like a blazing ball of Fire
    You snuck in when our backs where turn
    Causing disaster wherever you went
    Taking Lives every chance you got
    Didn't care if it was a man, woman, or child
    Changing lives forever
    Keeping us from family and friends
    Trapping us indoors
    Got us all praying for relief
    You keep changing the rules
    Got the world in a pandemic
    Got a us praying you'll go away
    And never come back again
    Got us fighting for normal life
    We won't let you win

How can I win

How can I win
    The heart of the one I love
    How can I show my love
    How can I open their eyes
    To show them the pain I feel
    For loving them
    How my heart aches
    To be with them
    How I want nothing but to love them
    To make them happy
    To make them number one
    To show them how special they are to me
    How can I win
    When I'm nothing in their eyes
    How can I win
    When I'm burning up with love for them
    How can I win

My Darling wife

My sweet darling wife
    Your the reason for my long life
    With all the magic years we had
    The beautiful kids you gave me
    With to many grandkids to count
    You look the same as the day we meet
    Your kisses are sweet as ever
    You still got the body of a model
    Loving you more than ever
    I knew way back when that you were the one
    The angel god sent me
    To give me a taste of heaven
    My sweet loving angel
    I love you

Goodbye Wife

Hello life
   Goodbye wife
   Hello freedom
   Goodbye captivity
   Hello money
   Goodbye debt
   Hello joy
   Goodbye fights

Goodbye Husband
Hello freedom
Goodbye husband
Hello peace
Goodbye pain
Hello life
Goodbye prison
Hello truth
Goodbye lies
Work

Hello time
Goodbye work
Hello fun
Goodbye boss
Hello family
Goodbye co-works
Hello sleep
Goodbye night shift

Why work
Went from homework to work
I'm at a loss with this boss
Eight hours a day with little pay
How can this be i just want to flee
Working at a soda shop
why can't I stop
Have no skills but got to pay the bills
Now i'm tired why did I get fired

Bestfriend

B = is for big hearted
   E = is for elegant
   S = is for sidekick
   T = is for treasure
   F = is for fabulous
   R = is for radiant
   I = is for inspiring
   E = is for empowering
   N = is for nery
   D = is for devoted

Family

F = is for fantastic
    A = is for amazing
    M = is for magnificent
    I = is for inspiring
    L = is for loving
    Y = is for yours
    Perfect one

I knew you were the one for me
    Right from the start
    How do I make you see
    How canI win your heart
    Your perfect in every way
    You turn my world upside down
    Now I pray i'm ok
    I hope one day you will come around
    Your always on my mind
    Now I'm going crazy
    You're one of a kind
    You hold my heart in captivity
    You're beauty is out of this world
    You take my breath away with every touch
    Now I live in a dream world
    Needing you way to much
    Never meet anyone like you
    Thought I was confused
    My love for you is true
    When i'm with you I get aroused

You have a voice of a goddess
Got to have you as my wife
In my eyes your flawless
You won my heart
Now I know true love
We will never be apart
Now I have my beloved

My dream

Your the only one I want to be with
You're hands I want on me
All I can do is pleaded the fifth
Won't you be my honey bee
Give me a chance for romance
You will love what I got to give
So how about that chance
You make me feel alive
I will hold you tight
Kiss you long
With just one night
As we make out to our song
I will show you passion like never before
I promise you will be mine
As you beg for more
I will send chills up your spine
As we cuddle in bed
Wrapped together like pretzels
No words unsaid
Knowing that your special
No other way to be
Now can you see
All you need is me
So please don't flee
A night with me all your dreams will come true
Let's live this fantasy
Up to you to make our dreams come true
For you hold my heart in capacity
I can't help im obsessed

For this all comes naturally
Your my ecstasy
So let's become a family

Mother

M = is for maternal
   O = is for omnipotent
   T = is for tender hearted
   H = is for heavenly
   E = is for extraordinary
   R = is for radiant

Father

F = is for fearless
   A = is for adroit
   T = is for talented
   H = is for heroic
   E = is for extravagant
   R = is for respectable

Sister

S = is for spontaneous
   I = is for impeccable
   S = is for sarcastic
   T = is for trustworthy
   E = is for elegant
   R = is for radiant

Brother

B = is for big hearted
    R = is for respectable
    O = is for omniscient
    T = is for thrifty
    H = is for hunky
    E = is for eccentric
    R = is for rebellious

Obesity

Hello skinny
    Goodbye fat
    Hello weights
    Goodbye snacks
    Hello muscles
    Goodbye laziness
    Hello health
    Goodbye sickness
    Hello running
    Goodbye couch
    Hello veggies
    Goodbye burgers

Soulmate
S = is for sidekick that always by your side
O = stands for the one's promise that they will always be there
U = stands for the unique quality that we both have
L = stands for the lover's we became
M = stands for magnificent partners we are
A = stands for the alter ego we get
T = stands for the treasure we see in each other
E = stands for the elegance we see in each other

With all of these words and many more make up the perfect soulmate.The one you long to be with. Your heart's desire. The kindred soul that becomes your significant other.Is your playmate at heart.When your soulmate becomes your empowering, inspiring,and kindred spirit.

This is a true soulmate.

The window

I set looking out the window
    Watching life go by wondering if anyone notice
    That i'm not there
    I wonder if anyone cares
    If i'm alive or dead
    How many would be hurting
    How many would be sad
    As I set watching out the window
    Wondering if any of them love me
    The way I love them
    I wondered as I set in front of the window
    How many really see me
    Do they see the difference in me
    Can they tell i'm in pain
    That my heart is broken
    I wonder how many of them are broken too
    Wishing one day we will all be fine
    Wondering which will happen first
    That I fall apart and roll over and die
    Or do I fight this with all I got
    Until the day I will be good again
    Wondering if I got the strength
    To bring out the warrior to fight the pain
    Wondering if my loved one's
    Will be my rock and support
    And not give up on me like before
    Do they really care and love me
    Knowing if the shoe was on the other foot
    I would be there

The rock and strength pushing them to fight
Right by their side
For I am loyal and my love is true

True love

When I look at you i'm hypnotized
    You take my breath away
    Your beauty I try to memorise
    All I want to do is stay
    Never wanting to leave your side
    Can't stop the feeling I got for you
    Can't wait to be your bride
    The love I have for you is true
    I know this relationship is taboo
    I know that sounds crazy
    As we both get tattoos
    As our love becomes spicy
    You are my heart's desire
    Cupid hit me with his arrow
    I feel like i'm on fire
    Your my Romero
    I'm your Juliet
    You swept me off my feet
    Let's break a sweat
    While we bring the heat
    While we slip into the sheets
    You are my true love
    My love will never decrease
    You are my turtledove
    The Beast
    He thought I was cheating
    So he started beating
    He was my man
    When he raised his hand

I tired to take a stand
When he gave me a backhand
He gave me a couple of kicks
Ain't he a prick
He slammed me to the wall
Now I have to call
Now I hurt
Might have to go to court
Here comes the police
Now he's beginning for peace
He's in jail
Now asking for bail
He wants released
Because he's a beast
Now he's facing time
Since he cross the line
He's thinking twice
Since he's paying the price
He's asking for forgiveness
Now that is just useless
He finally admitted
Now that he's convicted
He's got five years
To face his fears
I won't get the third degree
Since he's in the pen
It will never happen again

My Child
My loving child
You are the light of my life
My precious gift from above
Now I can't imagine
My life without you
Your small tiny hands and feet
The cute tiny little noise
The smile that melts my heart
My life will never be the same
Since the day you came
From the sleepless nights
To the magical moments
You first steps your first words
Who taught me how to love
Right from the start
So thank you my loving child
For all the special moments you gave me

I am a Mother
I am a mother
I love my kids
I want my family
I play peek a boo
I see my future
I am a wife
I am afraid of loss
I am happy with my husband
I am nervous about life
I am a wife

I'm a Prisoner

I am a prisoner
    But not of the normal kind
    For I have no cell or bars
    There's only one who hold the key
    For I am a prisoner of the heart
    It truly belongs to one
    She's a special breed
    The only one that can handle me
    For I was out of control
    Until she walked in my life
    Showed me how to love
    Now i'm her prisoner
    Serving a life sentence
    With no chance of parole
    Now serving hard time
    As I grow softer
    Under her loving hand
    Guiding me through the day
    Having the power over me
    For the crimes I committed
    I never went to trail

Even though I've been convicted
    For she captured my heart
    Now I'm her inmate
    So glad she is my warden
    Watching over me like a guardian
    I am a prisoner of love

Loving her more and more
So happy she's in control

Don't know why

I don't know why I try
    To win your heart
    When all I do is cry
    I never want to be apart
    I just want to make you mine
    I will never understand
    You were born to be mine
    Why do I live in a dream land
    The thought of you make me trimble
    As you take my breath away
    Why does this cause so much pain
    When your always on display
    Your so elegant and fine
    Looking like a supermodel
    Can you see our hearts are entwined
    Why is this impossible
    Do you understand we are meant to be together
    How can I get you to see
    You know we will both be better
    So why do you flee

Wedding day

Bride all dressed in white
    Groom in his tuxedo
    Bride's maids all in the same kind of dress
    Bride's mother setting in the first ariel crying
    Father walking the bride down the ariel
    Bride and Groom saying their vows
    Preacher announcing the new married couple
    Going to the wedding reception
    The best man giving his speech
    The throwing of the bouguet
    Lots of music and wine
    The honeymoon suite
    A lovely night of passion
    As the new Mr. and Mrs.

I do

The day I said I do
    Changed my life forever
    For I got to be with you
    Now I am truly blessed
    So hard to believe this is real
    To be with an angel like you
    You make my life better
    Improved it in so many ways
    Now I' happy all the time
    As I hold you tight
    Seeing your beautiful face
    For the east of my life
    Having you love me
    Over everyone else
    Knowing that I am your special one
    That we will be together to the end
    So I have to say it again
    That I am truly blessed
    Being with you
    As we both said I do

Grandbaby

My little precious grandbaby
    So small and tiny
    Please don't cry
    I will spoil you rotten
    Who will never do any wrong
    I will protect you from turmoil
    As I will always sing your song
    Your growing up so fast
    Right before my eyes
    You give me a blast
    Never wanting you to cry
    Your getting big and wise
    Now that your in school
    Your changing before my eyes
    Your super cool
    Still so sweet and precious
    Always my lovely grandchild
    You will always have my love
    As I will always be by your side

The perfect girl

The room got quit as you walked in
For you beauty catches everyone's eyes
As we were looking at an angel
With your long flowing yellow hair
Those gorgeous blue eyes
That tight fitting black dress
From that moment on I could not stop
Thinking about you
Always on my mind
Wondering what your doing and where your at
Thinking About becoming your secret admirer
For your beauty I can't get off my mind
Looking like a supermodel
Knowing your the perfect ten
Your every mans dream
Your everyones fantasie

Secret Admirer

I'm the one you don't know
    That have been in love with you
    The secret that I kept
    Even when I was by your side
    With a smile on my face
    Just because I'm near you
    Sending you the flowers
    Along with some sweet delights
    Little love notes left everywhere
    For you to find
    Watching a smile come over your face
    As you get all the gifts
    Watching you try to figure it out
    Who could be doing all of this
    Showing you all the special affection
    Letting you know you are loved
    But to scared to be rejected
    Hoping for a miracle
    That you will figure it out
    That I am your secret admirer
    As you realize you love me to
    That I make you Happy
    My Superhero

Your always there for me
    Always generous to everyone
    You saved my puppy
    Standing up to bullies

Never seem to be in pain
Fight the monsters in my closet
You know everything
Always taking my pain away
Your my superhero
You have no special powers
I never seen you fly
You never shoot fire from your hands
But you don't need no super powers
For you are unique
One of a kind
You are a real crusader
Always my role model
The one I look up to
There's no one like you
You are my dad

My mom

You gave me life
    Held my hand as I learned to walk
    Wiped away my tears
    Kissing all my boo's
    Holding me on your lap
    Tucking me in my bed
    Baking me cookies to eat
    Playing with me all the time
    Watching all my favorite cartoons
    Singing all my favorite songs
    Helping me with my homework
    Teaching me to play ball
    Making sure I brushed my teeth
    Always getting me to eat my veggies
    Teaching me to be strong
    For you are very special to me
    Your my loving mom

Secret Romance

Cute little nicknames
Sweet little texts
Secret telephone calls
Mystery dates out
Trying to keep the secret
Grabbing kisses where we can
Precious little gifts
Special moment with each other
Going on for months
Can't keep our hands off of each other
Late night visits
Steamy hot passion
Wild luxurious dinners
Our secret romance

Workouts

Doing several squats
    Different kinds of lunges
    Yoga on the beach
    Pilates in the living room
    Long hikes on trails
    Climbing all those stairs
    Hour long spinning classes
    Mild morning runs
    Couple of hours of boxing
    These crazy dumbbells
    Working on our ads
    Breaking a sweat
    Working out our muscles
    Working the whole body
    Pain all over
    Warm up and cool downs
    Lots of reps and sets
    Physical exhausting workouts
    Personal fitness trainers

Special Love

We were strangers
	That became roommates
	That grew in be bestfriends
	Then we became a family
	But there was more going on
	You was stealing my heart
	As time went on
	The special way you treated me
	The sweet way you talked
	Drew me in closer to you
	That crazy way you made me feel
	When I was with you
	Never felt like this before
	I was told it was true love
	That my heart belongs to you
	You hold the key to my future
	Without me knowing it
	You secretly stole my heart
	For I am in love with you

One of a kind love

You send me flowers
	Give me chocolates
	Take me out to eat
	Going on shopping trips
	Special little nicknames
	Sweet love notes
	Always holding hands
	Long lasting kisses
	Sexy phone calls
	Late night chats
	Early morning drinks
	A shoulder to cry on
	Being special to me
	Loving me like no other
	Showing me passion
	Taking care of me
	Unforgettable kisses
	Remarkable nights
	Incredible days
	Loving you

Wedding day 2

W = is for the way we worship each other
E = is for our everlasting love
D = is for the dedication we have
D = is us declaring our love
I = is the way I idolize you
N = is for the nervous we share
G = is the genuine affection we have

D = is the desire we have for each other
A = is for how we adore each other
Y = is for the yearning I have for you

One's true love

O = is the object of affection
　　N = is for nuzzles
　　E = is for endearment
　　S = is for sweet love

T = is for tenderness
　　R = is for romance
　　U = is for the urges
　　E = is for enmity

L = is for the lust
　　O = is for the obsession
　　V = is for value
　　E = is for erotic

Man's best friend

M = is for mischievous
  A = is for affectionate
  N = is for naughty
  S = is for spoiled

B = is for beloved
  E = is for eager to please
  S = is for snuggly
  T = is for territorial
  F = is for four legged
  R = is for rambunctious
  I = is for intelligent
  E = is for energetic
  N = is for neutered
  D = is for devoted

I am a Husband

I am a son
    I love my wife
    I want a long life
    I play with my kids
    I see my parents
    I am a father
    I am afraid of devorce
    I am happy with my family is together
    I am nervous of the future
    I am excited for my babys
    I am a husband

Goodbye School

Hello career
 Goodbye school
 Hello boss
 Goodbye teacher
 Hello workdays
 Goodbye people
 Hello paychecks
 Goodbye allowance
 Hello first house
 Goodbye parents house
 Hello late nights
 Goodbye curfew

Our family reunion

O = is for overjoyed
    U = is for up beat
    R = is for ray of sunshine
    F = is for farewells
    A = is for adventurous
    M = is for mental health
    I = is for imagination
    L = is for love
    Y = is for your family
    R = is for rumbustious
    E = is for emotional
    U = is for the ups and downs
    N = is for normal
    I = is for infelicitous
    O = is for offspring
    N = is for next of kin

Our relationship

O = is for oneness
    U = is for understanding
    R = is for respect

R = is for real
    E = is for everlasting
    L = is for love
    A = is for amazing
    T = is for tenderness
    I = is for intimate
    O = is for orgasmic
    N= is for nearly
    S = is for sexual
    H = is for honest
    I = is for intense
    P = is for positive

About the Author

Katharine L Niffen is an aspiring aurhor with a lot of passion for writing.Who loves to make people smile .She is a doughter, she is a single mother ,a loving grandma.